ANAESTHETICS

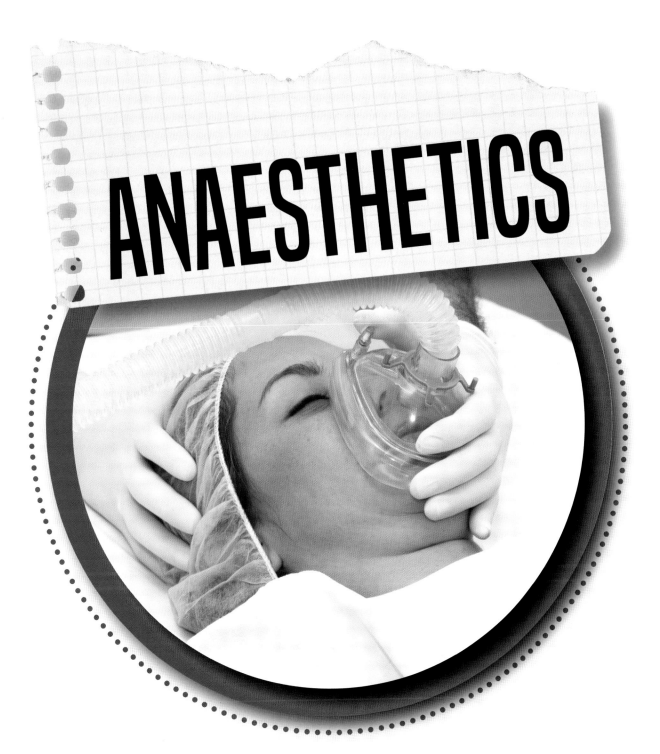

By Joanna Brundle

BookLife
PUBLISHING

©2019
BookLife Publishing Ltd.
King's Lynn
Norfolk PE30 4LS

All rights reserved.
Printed in Malaysia.

A catalogue record for this book is
available from the British Library.

ISBN: 978-1-78637-541-4

Written by:
Joanna Brundle

Edited by:
Kirsty Holmes

Designed by:
Dan Scase

All facts, statistics, web addresses
and URLs in this book were verified
as valid and accurate at time of
writing. No responsibility for any
changes to external websites or
references can be accepted by
either the author or publisher.

PHOTO CREDITS

Front Cover – Oxy_gen, Leone_V, herjua, BLACKDAY, Sunflowerr, StudioAz, vector toon, Sylfida, Anna Violet. 2 – Diego Cervo. 4 – Sergey Ryzhov. 5 – Gorodenkoff, Olena Yakobchuk. 6 – herjua. 7 – Dmytro Zinkevych, JPC-PROD. 8 – Juri Pozzi, Toong Stockers, Lasse_Sven, Stock Vector. 9 – Oxana Gracheva, Kate Vigdis. 10 – Georgios Kollidas, Nicku. 11 – unoL. 12 – Everett - Art, VectorMine. 13 – Everett Historical. 14 – Marzolino, jorisvo, Maike Hildebrandt. 15 – edwardolive, Syda Productions. 16 – fabiodevilla. 17 – Monkey Business Images, Sakurra. 18 – Syda Productions, Romaset. 19 – Chaikom, Alexander Raths. 20 – Anneka. 21 – Marcin Balcerza, Valua Vitaly. 22 – VectorMine. 23 – royaltystockphoto.com, Pitju, Jolygon. 24 – Dan Race, Dmitry Kalinovsky. 25 – KieferPix, Romaset, Anan Kaewkhammul, Olesia Bilkei. 26 – Tunatura, Siyanight. 27 – beerkoff, FamVeld. 28 – LEDOMSTOCK. 30 – Numstocker. Borders on all pages – Leone_V. Antibiotic vectors throughout – Oxy_gen. Ripped paper throughout – BLACKDAY. Heart rate vector – StudioAz. Logo heart – vector toon. Images are courtesy of Shutterstock.com. With thanks to Getty Images, Thinkstock Photo and iStockphoto.

LIFE-SAVING SCIENCE

Words that look like **THIS** can be found in the glossary on page 31.

THE WORLD OF MEDICINE

Every day, millions of people around the world suffer from minor and serious illnesses and receive treatment for them. They may have become infected with a disease, had an accident or been admitted to hospital for routine or emergency treatment. They are looked after by **HEALTHCARE PROFESSIONALS** who have been trained to give the care they need. Patients rely on these professionals and the treatments they give to return them to full health. Sometimes, medical problems are life-threatening, but a huge range of life-saving medicines and treatments are available to healthcare professionals to help them find and treat medical problems. Anaesthetics (say: ann-as-THET-iks) are an example of this kind of life-saving miracle.

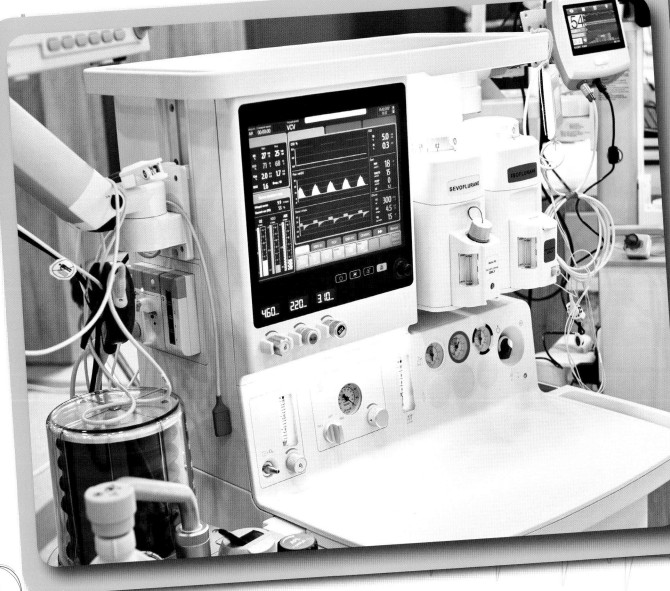

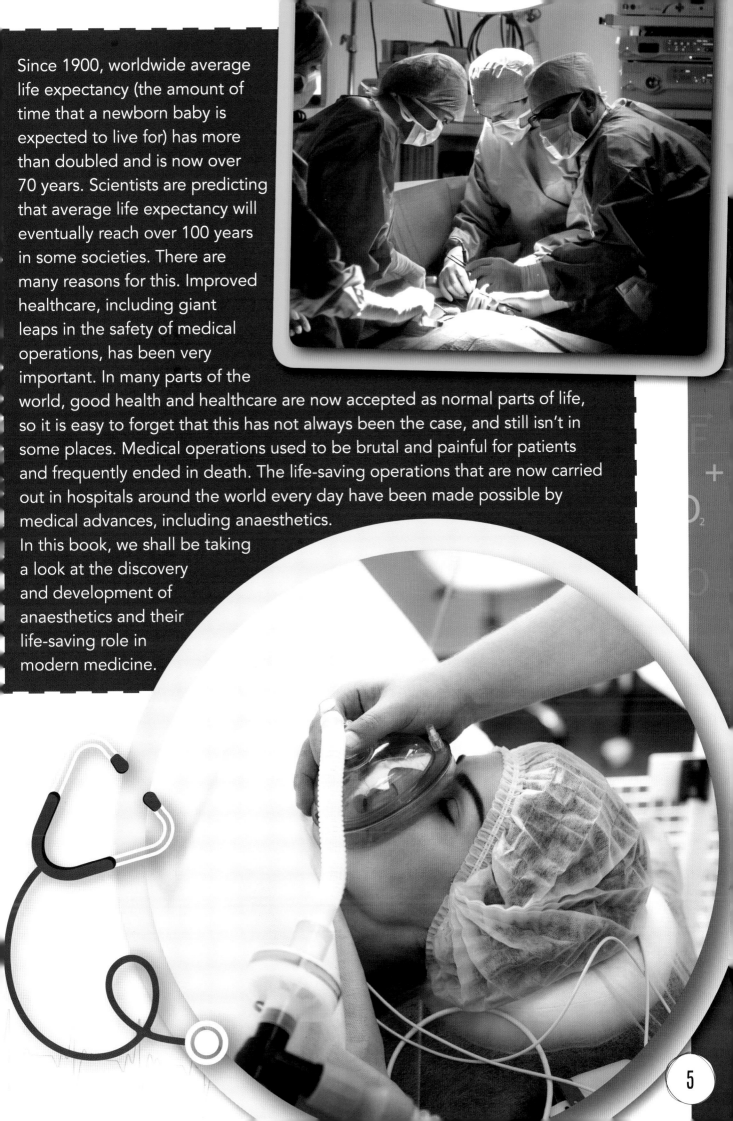

Since 1900, worldwide average life expectancy (the amount of time that a newborn baby is expected to live for) has more than doubled and is now over 70 years. Scientists are predicting that average life expectancy will eventually reach over 100 years in some societies. There are many reasons for this. Improved healthcare, including giant leaps in the safety of medical operations, has been very important. In many parts of the world, good health and healthcare are now accepted as normal parts of life, so it is easy to forget that this has not always been the case, and still isn't in some places. Medical operations used to be brutal and painful for patients and frequently ended in death. The life-saving operations that are now carried out in hospitals around the world every day have been made possible by medical advances, including anaesthetics. In this book, we shall be taking a look at the discovery and development of anaesthetics and their life-saving role in modern medicine.

WHAT ARE ANAESTHETICS?

Anaesthetics are medications given to patients before and during medical tests or operations. They are sometimes used to prevent or reduce pain during a procedure when the patient is awake. They are also used to put the patient into a deep sleep, so that the patient feels no pain during the procedure and does not remember it afterwards. Anaesthetics can also be used to **SEDATE** patients, so that they feel calm and comfortable during tests or procedures that might otherwise be uncomfortable. Anaesthetics can be given by an injection or by inhalation (breathing in) of gases, using a face mask. Sometimes, an anaesthetic cream is applied to numb an area where an injection is to be given. The state of not being able to feel pain is called anaesthesia (say: ann-as-THEE-sha).

A face mask is used to administer anaesthetic gases.

FACT

THE WORDS 'ANAESTHETICS' AND 'ANAESTHESIA' COME FROM TWO GREEK WORDS — 'AN' MEANING 'WITHOUT' AND 'AESTHESIS' MEANING 'SENSATION OR FEELING'.

Most people have an anaesthetic at some point in their lives. It may involve the numbing of a small area using an injection, for example by a dentist. Maybe you have had milk teeth removed by a dentist using this type of anaesthetic? Longer, more serious operations require the patient to be put to sleep. Have you or someone you know had this type of anaesthetic, for example to remove tonsils or an appendix? Whatever type of anaesthetic is given, the effect is temporary. The patient will regain sensation (feeling) and, if they have been asleep, will wake up when the anaesthetic drugs are stopped.

Dentists may give an anaesthetic injection before removing or filling a tooth.

ANAESTHETISTS

Anaesthetists are fully-qualified doctors who have completed several more years of special training in anaesthetics. They administer anaesthetic drugs and look after a patient before, during and after **SURGERY** or tests. Some anaesthetists are specially trained to care for children. They are known as as paediatric (say: pee-dee-at-trick) anaesthetists.

FACT

IN THE UK ALONE, AROUND 3·5 MILLION PEOPLE (1 IN 20) HAVE AN ANAESTHETIC EACH YEAR.

Paediatric anaesthetists have completed extra training to help them look after children.

MEDICINE BEFORE ANAESTHETICS

Acupuncture is still used today for pain relief, but many doctors are not sure if it is effective.

Before the introduction of anaesthetics, operations that are now carried out routinely and safely were extremely painful for the patient. They were very risky too, frequently resulting in death. Patients were often given something hard, such as a leather strap or piece of wood, to bite on. They sometimes had to be held down to allow the **SURGEON** to carry out the operation without them moving. Surgeons had to be able to operate very quickly if there was to be any chance of the patient recovering. An ancient treatment called acupuncture was used by Chinese doctors to try to anaesthetise their patients. Acupuncture involves the use of very fine needles to encourage the body to produce pain-relieving substances called endorphins. An ancient Italian practice was to cover the patient's head with a wooden bowl and beat on it repeatedly until the patient became unconscious. In medieval England, a substance called dwale was used as an anaesthetic. The recipe included lettuce, vinegar and a poisonous plant called belladonna or deadly nightshade.

DEADLY NIGHTSHADE

A drug called alcohol was commonly used to sedate patients or make them unconscious. Another drug called opium and a plant known as mandrake were also used. Opium is a reddish-brown, heavily scented substance that slows down the 'pain messages' travelling between the body and the brain. It is prepared from a milky juice obtained from the seed heads of a poppy (Papaver somniferum) traditionally grown in Asia. Mandrake is a medicinal plant with a fleshy root whose shape resembles the human body. It has sedative properties and has been used as an anaesthetic since Roman times. Before having surgery, patients were given a piece of the plant's root to chew.

POPPY SEED HEADS

The human-looking mandrake root was believed to have magical powers.

FACT

MANDRAKES APPEAR IN HARRY POTTER AND THE CHAMBER OF SECRETS, AND HARRY POTTER AND THE DEATHLY HALLOWS — SEE IF YOU CAN FIND OUT WHERE!

DR SEISHU HANAOKA

A Japanese surgeon, Dr Seishu Hanaoka (1760–1835), produced an anaesthetic mixture of herbal substances that he called tsusensan (say: sue-SEN-san). In October 1804, after many experiments on animals, he used tsusensan to carry out the first successful operation in the world on a human patient using a general anaesthetic – one that puts the patient to sleep.

O_2

THE DISCOVERY OF ANAESTHETICS

In 1772, English chemist Joseph Priestley (1733–1804) discovered the gas **NITROUS OXIDE**. Another English chemist, Humphrey Davy (1778–1829), studied this gas and, in 1799, published his findings, which showed that when inhaled, nitrous oxide eased pain. Davy suggested the use of nitrous oxide in surgery. British scientist Michael Faraday (1791–1867), who became famous for his experiments with electricity, was taken on as Davy's assistant. In 1818, Faraday published his findings that inhaling **ETHER** caused sleepiness and pain relief. As often happens with scientific discoveries, however, it was a long time before either discovery was put to practical use. In 1844, the story moved to the US, where a travelling showman called Gardner Quincy Colton drew large crowds, demonstrating the effects of inhaling nitrous oxide. Horace Wells (1815–1848), a local dentist, was in the audience. He was fascinated.

Joseph Priestley is best known for his discovery of <u>OXYGEN</u> in 1774.

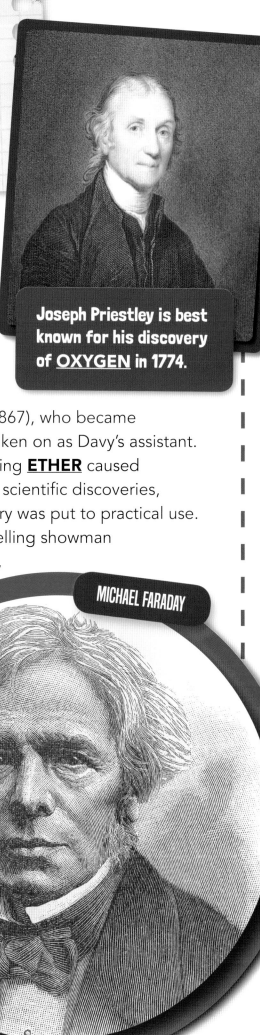

MICHAEL FARADAY

FACT

DAVY DISCOVERED THAT INHALING NITROUS OXIDE MADE HIM LAUGH, SO HE NICKNAMED IT 'LAUGHING GAS', A TERM THAT IS STILL USED TODAY.

Wells had learnt how to make dentures (false teeth) and had been searching for a way to remove a patient's rotten teeth painlessly. He thought that nitrous oxide might be the answer. He learnt how to make the gas and proved its effectiveness by having one of his own teeth removed and by giving public demonstrations. Wells' colleague, a dentist and medical student named William T. G. Morton, realised that inhaling ether might also prove an effective anaesthetic and began experiments. In October 1846, he successfully administered ether to a patient, Gilbert Abbott, allowing a surgeon, Dr John Warren, to remove a growth from the man's neck without pain. It was a major breakthrough and details of this success spread rapidly. By December 1846, the exciting news had reached the United Kingdom. Dr Robert Liston (1794–1847), a leading London surgeon, watched the painless removal of a tooth from a young lady, Miss Lonsdale, using ether inhalation, by Dr Francis Boott.

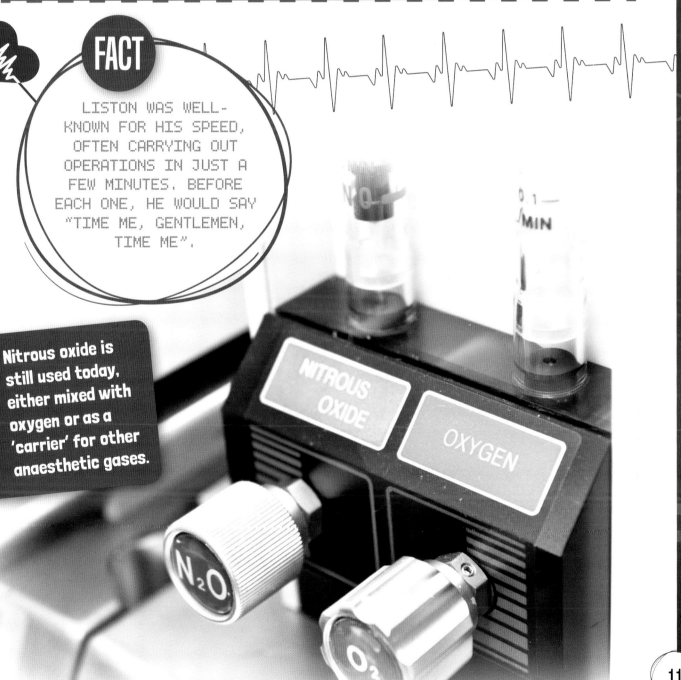

FACT

LISTON WAS WELL-KNOWN FOR HIS SPEED, OFTEN CARRYING OUT OPERATIONS IN JUST A FEW MINUTES. BEFORE EACH ONE, HE WOULD SAY "TIME ME, GENTLEMEN, TIME ME".

Nitrous oxide is still used today, either mixed with oxygen or as a 'carrier' for other anaesthetic gases.

Queen Victoria famously hated being pregnant and the pain of childbirth, so she was keen to try out chloroform.

Liston was impressed by what he had seen and immediately arranged to carry out the first public demonstration of surgery using ether in the UK. It was a success and a further breakthrough. James 'Young' Simpson (1811–1870), a Scottish surgeon and **OBSTETRICIAN** (say: ob-steh-TRISH-an), happened to be on an annual visit to London at the time. He too was enthusiastic about the use of anaesthetics, particularly for women experiencing labour pains in childbirth. The following year, in 1847, Simpson was experimenting with various chemicals with two friends and accidentally discovered the anaesthetic properties of another substance, called chloroform. Chloroform is a colourless, **VOLATILE** liquid that can daze or knock people out, even in very small doses. Following the successful use of chloroform in a dental procedure in Edinburgh, Simpson began to use it as an anaesthetic in childbirth. John Snow, a London doctor, quickly became an expert in the use of chloroform. He successfully administered it to Queen Victoria for the births of her last two children, Prince Leopold in 1853 and Princess Beatrice in 1857.

FACT

IN HIGH DOSES, CHLOROFORM CAN KILL. IT IS NOT USED AS AN ANAESTHETIC TODAY, BECAUSE IT IS VERY DIFFICULT TO GIVE THE CORRECT DOSAGE TO ACHIEVE AN ANAESTHETIC EFFECT WITHOUT KILLING THE PATIENT.

After the death of John Snow, another English doctor, Joseph Clover (1825–1882), began to develop new and safer ways of administering chloroform and other inhaled anaesthetics. He invented several pieces of **APPARATUS** that allowed him to administer a safe and controlled amount of the drugs. His 'portable regulating ether inhaler' combined a face mask, a chamber for the ether and a water jacket to prevent the ether from cooling. It remained in use by anaesthetists until well into the 20th century. Clover also realised that it might be safer to give a mixture of drugs in lower doses, rather than a much larger, and perhaps **TOXIC**, dose of a single drug. His skill meant that, by 1871, he had anaesthetised around 13,000 patients without a single death. His patients included many famous public figures, such as Florence Nightingale (1820–1910) and British Prime Minister Robert Peel (1788–1850).

Florence Nightingale (1820–1910) was the founder of modern nursing, famously introducing proper care for soldiers injured during the **CRIMEAN WAR**.

CHCl₃

This illustration of a battle in the Crimean War gives an idea of the fierce fighting that led to so many serious injuries.

The popularity of anaesthetics continued to grow, thanks not only to royal patients but also to their use on the battlefield. During the Crimean War, thousands of soldiers suffered terrible injuries, but anaesthetics allowed many to have the life-saving surgery they needed. But not everyone thought anaesthetics were a good idea. Some religious groups claimed that pain, for example in childbirth, was natural and necessary. They argued that, like other forms of suffering, it was an important part of our lives and had spiritual meaning. Some people thought that inhaled drugs were dangerous after reports of explosions of stored drugs in the 1840s and 1850s. Others thought that criminals might use ether or chloroform to overpower their victims. It was also reported that, before the abolition of slavery in the US in 1865, some surgeons acted improperly by practising anaesthesia on slaves.

Religious campaigners used a quotation from the Bible "In sorrow thou shalt bring forth children" to argue against the use of anaesthetics in childbirth.

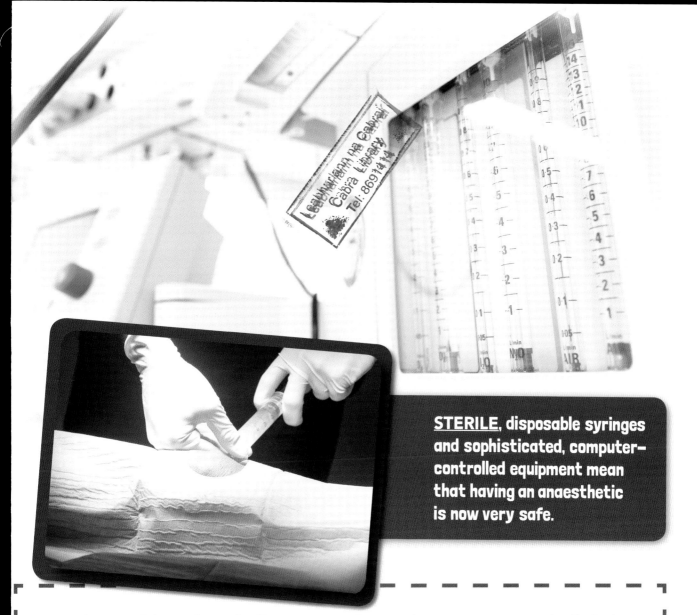

STERILE, disposable syringes and sophisticated, computer-controlled equipment mean that having an anaesthetic is now very safe.

As evidence of the safe and effective use of anaesthetics grew, it gradually led to their acceptance and routine use in medicine. The use of effective anaesthetics meant that surgeons no longer had to be quick and brutal. Instead, they could take their time to operate with skill and care. In 1942, substances that produce relaxation of muscles were introduced. This advance allowed breathing tubes to be inserted into the patient's **WINDPIPE**. In 1948, the first modern local anaesthetic (one that anaesthetises only a particular area) was introduced. It was called lidocaine. By the 1950s, all the ideas on which modern anaesthesia are based were in place and modern anaesthetic drugs are largely improvements of those available then. During the 1970s and 1980s, however, a Scottish vet, Dr John Glen, discovered and developed propofol. Propofol soon became popular because it is a fast-acting anaesthetic and patients recover quickly from its effects. It is now the world's most widely-used anaesthetic.

FACT

IN 2016, THE **WORLD HEALTH ORGANIZATION** CLASSED PROPOFOL AS AN 'ESSENTIAL MEDICINE'. AT THAT TIME, MORE THAN 190 MILLION PEOPLE HAD BEEN GIVEN PROPOFOL.

DIFFERENT TYPES OF ANAESTHETICS

GENERAL ANAESTHETICS

A general anaesthetic puts a patient into an **INDUCED COMA**, so that they cannot feel pain or respond to any other **STIMULUS**. Patients under general anaesthetic cannot move and are also unable to form memories, so that when they wake up, they have no memory of the operation. Although the term 'sleep' is often used, being under a general anaesthetic is very different from being asleep. Someone who is asleep may still move about in bed and may even speak. They can respond to a stimulus such as pain, a loud noise or being too hot or too cold, and will wake up on their own.

WHEN ARE GENERAL ANAESTHETICS USED?

General anaesthetics are used if the procedure:

- Will take a long time
- Will affect the patient's breathing
- Involves a major **ORGAN** such as the heart or lungs
- Could make the patient lose a lot of blood
- Involves a large area of the body
- Is being carried out in an emergency

Serious road traffic accidents may result in injuries that need emergency treatment under a general anaesthetic.

WHAT HAPPENS BEFORE A GENERAL ANAESTHETIC IS GIVEN?

A patient often meets the anaesthetist before an operation to talk about what will happen and the best anaesthetic to use. The anaesthetist asks the patient about their **LIFESTYLE**, any medications that they are already taking and whether they have any **ALLERGIES**. The family history of the patient is also checked. This is to see if anyone else in the family has experienced problems, such as an allergic reaction, when having an anaesthetic.

If a general anaesthetic is required, the patient must not eat for six to eight hours before the procedure. Water is allowed until two hours before. Patients who are anxious about having their operation are sometimes given a pre-med (short for pre-medication) about an hour before the procedure. This is a medicine, or mixture of medicines, that makes the patient feel sleepy and relaxed.

IN THE OPERATING THEATRE

A liquid anaesthetic is injected into a vein, often in the back of the hand, through a cannula. A cannula is a thin, flexible, plastic tube. The patient is sometimes asked to count backwards from ten but is usually asleep very quickly. A face mask is used for inhaled gases.

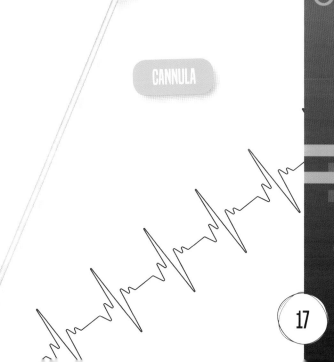

CANNULA

GENERAL ANAESTHETICS FOR CHILDREN

Children are often given a pre-med. It can be a bit painful to have the anaesthetic injection so special anaesthetic cream known as 'magic cream' is often used to numb the place to be injected. If a face mask is needed, different flavoured masks are available and the child can choose their favourite flavour. A parent or carer is usually allowed to stay with their child until the child is asleep.

WHAT HAPPENS DURING THE PROCEDURE?

Anaesthetists use sophisticated technology like this but also use their eyes, ears and hands to watch their patients and to listen to and feel their breathing, pulse and temperature.

Once the patient is asleep, the anaesthetist might put a tube through the patient's mouth into the windpipe. This is to help the patient to breathe and to ensure that they have enough oxygen throughout procedure. Special equipment is used to monitor the patient's **HEART RATE**, temperature, blood pressure and the oxygen levels in the blood. The patient's level of **CONSCIOUSNESS** is monitored throughout. The anaesthetist monitors the **CARBON DIOXIDE** in each breath that the patient exhales. The amount of blood that the heart is pumping is also closely monitored. The anaesthetist uses all these readings to adjust the medications being given so that the patient remains pain-free and asleep.

A pulse oximeter (say: ox-imm-ih-tuh) is a small clip-like device that is attached to a finger, toe or ear lobe and is used in all operations to monitor oxygen levels.

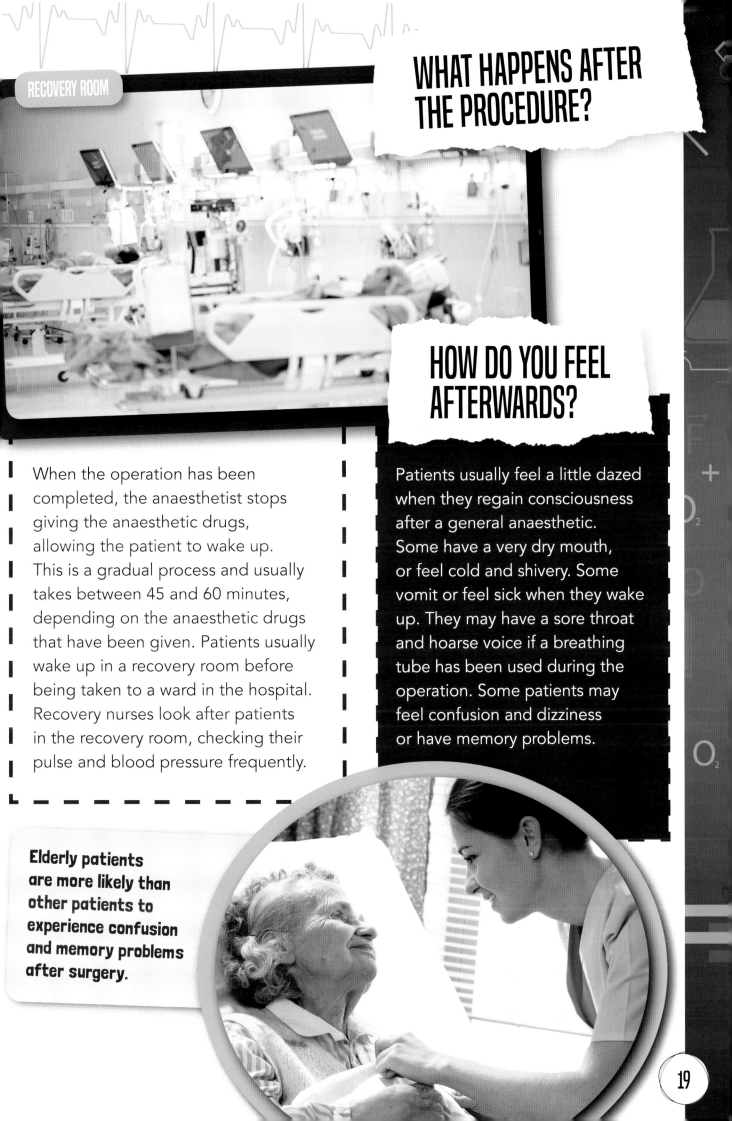

WHAT HAPPENS AFTER THE PROCEDURE?

HOW DO YOU FEEL AFTERWARDS?

When the operation has been completed, the anaesthetist stops giving the anaesthetic drugs, allowing the patient to wake up. This is a gradual process and usually takes between 45 and 60 minutes, depending on the anaesthetic drugs that have been given. Patients usually wake up in a recovery room before being taken to a ward in the hospital. Recovery nurses look after patients in the recovery room, checking their pulse and blood pressure frequently.

Patients usually feel a little dazed when they regain consciousness after a general anaesthetic. Some have a very dry mouth, or feel cold and shivery. Some vomit or feel sick when they wake up. They may have a sore throat and hoarse voice if a breathing tube has been used during the operation. Some patients may feel confusion and dizziness or have memory problems.

Elderly patients are more likely than other patients to experience confusion and memory problems after surgery.

REGIONAL ANAESTHETICS

A regional anaesthetic involves numbing only the part of the body that is being operated on, for example a leg or arm. This type of anaesthetic is also known as a 'block'. The patient remains conscious throughout, but can choose whether to be fully awake or to be given a sedative medication to make them feel relaxed and sleepy. Different types of regional anaesthetic can be used.

SPINAL BLOCK

This type of block involves inserting a needle into the patient's back. A single anaesthetic injection is given into the fluid that surrounds the **SPINAL CORD**. The needle is then removed. A spinal block anaesthetises the lower abdomen (belly), the pelvis and both legs. Its numbing effects usually last for around two to four hours. A spinal block is often used in orthopaedic operations – those involving bone and muscle problems.

An epidural is very similar to a spinal block but, rather than the needle being removed, a fine plastic tube remains inserted into the lower back. This allows the anaesthetic drug to be 'topped up' if necessary. Epidurals are often used in operations involving the legs and to relieve pain in childbirth. They can also be used for operations involving the chest or abdomen. In this case, the needle is inserted higher up to numb the correct area.

Some mums-to-be have an epidural for the birth of their baby.

PERIPHERAL NERVE BLOCKS

Peripheral nerve blocks are used to numb the nerves supplying a particular part of the body, such as the hand, foot or lower leg. The anaesthetic is injected very close to the nerves that supply the particular body part. In order for this type of block to work effectively, the anaesthetic must be injected accurately into exactly the right spot. Pinpointing the right spot is sometimes done using a machine that sends a mild electric charge that causes the muscles to twitch. Sometimes, an ultrasound scan, also called a sonogram, is used. Ultrasound is a procedure that uses special sound waves to create an image on a screen of the inside of the body part that is to be injected.

Ultrasound produces a clear image on the monitor of the inside of the body part.

LOCAL ANAESTHETICS

Some minor procedures do not require either a general or regional anaesthetic. In these cases, an injection is given underneath the skin, numbing a very small, localised area. This is called a local anaesthetic. The patient feels no pain in the injected area, but can still feel movement or pressure. Local anaesthetics are normally given by doctors or dentists, but some mild local anaesthetics can be bought or dispensed with a prescription at a **PHARMACY**.

FACT

LOCAL ANAESTHETICS CAN ALSO BE USED TO TREAT LONG-TERM PAINFUL CONDITIONS SUCH AS BACK OR JOINT PAIN.

Gels or sprays used to treat mouth ulcers or sore throats are mild local anaesthetics that can be bought at a pharmacy.

HOW DO ANAESTHETICS WORK?

The human central nervous system is made up of the brain and spinal cord. The peripheral nervous system is made up of nerve fibres that spread out from the spinal cord to all parts of the body, from the top of the head to the tips of the toes. Sensory receptors are special **PROTEINS** found on body **CELLS**. Their job is to pick up signals on the outside of the cell. Sensory receptors send messages via the nerve fibres to the spinal cord and from there to the brain. The brain processes the messages and sends out instructions to the body in the form of nerve impulses. If, for example, we pick up something hot, messages travel from the hand to the brain, which registers pain and sends back messages to pull the hand away. In this way, pain is very important for our survival.

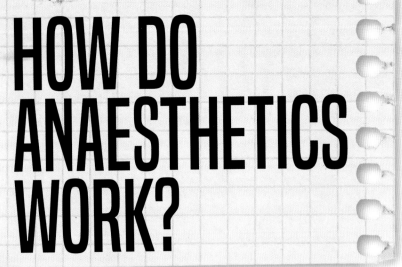

PERIPHERAL NERVOUS SYSTEM

BRAIN

PERIPHERAL NERVOUS SYSTEM

SPINAL CORD

PERIPHERAL NERVOUS SYSTEM

FACT

THERE ARE DIFFERENT SENSORY RECEPTORS FOR DIFFERENT KINDS OF PAIN, FOR EXAMPLE PAINFUL, DANGEROUS HEAT.

CENTRAL NERVOUS SYSTEM (CNS)

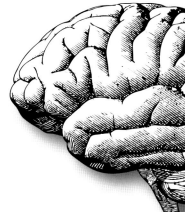

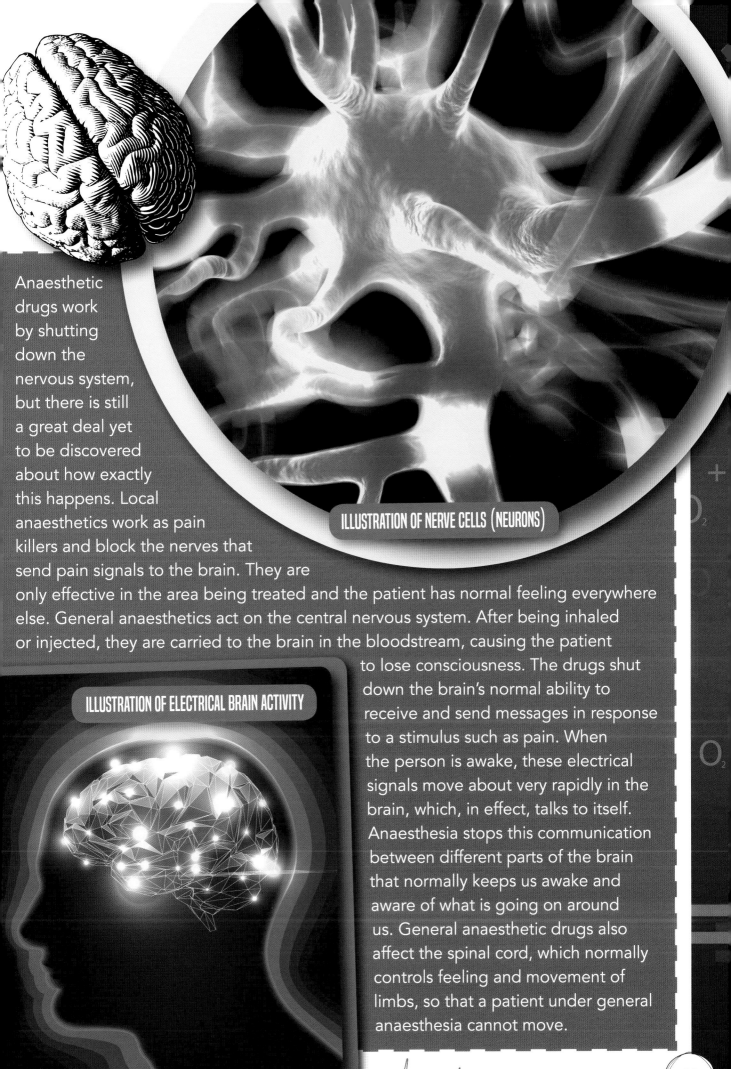

Anaesthetic drugs work by shutting down the nervous system, but there is still a great deal yet to be discovered about how exactly this happens. Local anaesthetics work as pain killers and block the nerves that send pain signals to the brain. They are only effective in the area being treated and the patient has normal feeling everywhere else. General anaesthetics act on the central nervous system. After being inhaled or injected, they are carried to the brain in the bloodstream, causing the patient to lose consciousness. The drugs shut down the brain's normal ability to receive and send messages in response to a stimulus such as pain. When the person is awake, these electrical signals move about very rapidly in the brain, which, in effect, talks to itself. Anaesthesia stops this communication between different parts of the brain that normally keeps us awake and aware of what is going on around us. General anaesthetic drugs also affect the spinal cord, which normally controls feeling and movement of limbs, so that a patient under general anaesthesia cannot move.

ILLUSTRATION OF NERVE CELLS (NEURONS)

ILLUSTRATION OF ELECTRICAL BRAIN ACTIVITY

USES OF ANAESTHETICS

HUMAN ORGAN

Anaesthetics that sedate the patient while they are awake allow tests to be carried out that would otherwise be too uncomfortable. An example is endoscopy, a procedure in which a tiny camera is used to check a patient's digestive system (gut).

Anaesthetics allow surgeons to carry out every kind of operation, without the patient feeling pain. Even very long operations, such as the **TRANSPLANTATION** of a heart or lungs, can be carried out safely, thanks to effective anaesthetics.

Endoscopy is an example of a procedure that would be difficult and uncomfortable without the use of sedative anaesthetics.

Local anaesthetics allow minor procedures to be carried out quickly and safely. Examples include removal of verrucas or warts, minor skin surgery and dental treatments. Local anaesthetics are also used in eye surgery, such as laser treatment to correct defective vision or to remove a **CATARACT**. This type of anaesthetic is also used to carry out a biopsy – the removal of a small sample from the body for examination under a **MICROSCOPE**.

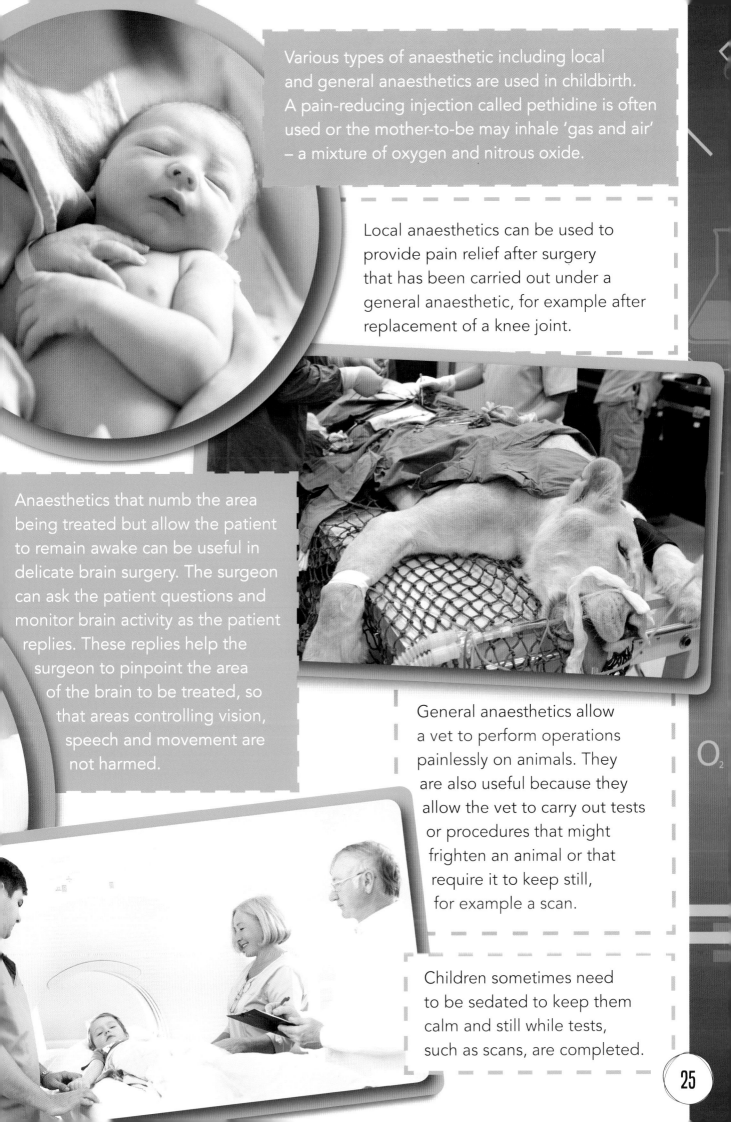

Various types of anaesthetic including local and general anaesthetics are used in childbirth. A pain-reducing injection called pethidine is often used or the mother-to-be may inhale 'gas and air' – a mixture of oxygen and nitrous oxide.

Local anaesthetics can be used to provide pain relief after surgery that has been carried out under a general anaesthetic, for example after replacement of a knee joint.

Anaesthetics that numb the area being treated but allow the patient to remain awake can be useful in delicate brain surgery. The surgeon can ask the patient questions and monitor brain activity as the patient replies. These replies help the surgeon to pinpoint the area of the brain to be treated, so that areas controlling vision, speech and movement are not harmed.

General anaesthetics allow a vet to perform operations painlessly on animals. They are also useful because they allow the vet to carry out tests or procedures that might frighten an animal or that require it to keep still, for example a scan.

Children sometimes need to be sedated to keep them calm and still while tests, such as scans, are completed.

RISKS AND SIDE EFFECTS OF ANAESTHETICS

Anaesthetics are very safe for most people. This is thanks to the skill of highly-trained anaesthetists and to the specialist equipment and range of drugs available to them. As with all medical procedures, however, there are risks involved with having an anaesthetic. It is possible to have an allergic reaction to anaesthetic drugs, for example. This may vary from a mild reaction such as a rash, to a serious life-threatening reaction called anaphylaxis. Some patients may also be allergic to antibiotics used or to equipment made of **LATEX**, for example surgical gloves. There is also a very small risk of death under general anaesthetic – only one in 100,000 patients dies.

FACT

SIGNS OF AN ANAPHYLACTIC REACTION INCLUDE LOW BLOOD PRESSURE, SKIN SWELLING AND RASH AND SWELLING OF THE INSIDE OF THE THROAT.

RISK FACTORS FOR A GENERAL ANAESTHETIC

- Being a smoker
- Being overweight
- Having high blood pressure
- Having an existing medical problem such as diabetes, epilepsy or disease of the heart, lungs or kidneys
- Being elderly
- Having an emergency operation
- Having major, lengthy surgery

Anaesthetists monitor patients closely to make sure they stay asleep and pain-free throughout their operation. Occasionally, however, a patient wakes up during surgery. This is called anaesthetic awareness. Afterwards, the patient may be able to remember their surroundings in the operating theatre or what was said by doctors. Anaesthetic awareness can be frightening because the patient cannot move or tell the surgeon they are awake. Fortunately, it is very rare. Anaesthetic awareness has been shown to be most likely to affect women, young adults and patients who abuse alcohol and non-medical drugs.

Anaesthetists monitor patients very closely.

SIDE EFFECTS

Side effects are unwanted extra effects of a medication or treatment. As well as the side effects described on page 19, some patients also have itchy skin, headaches and bruising or soreness where they have been injected. Side effects usually disappear quickly on their own. Some patients may have damage to their teeth or bruising to the mouth and lips, caused by a breathing tube. Patients who have had a local anaesthetic may feel a tingly sensation as the medication wears off.

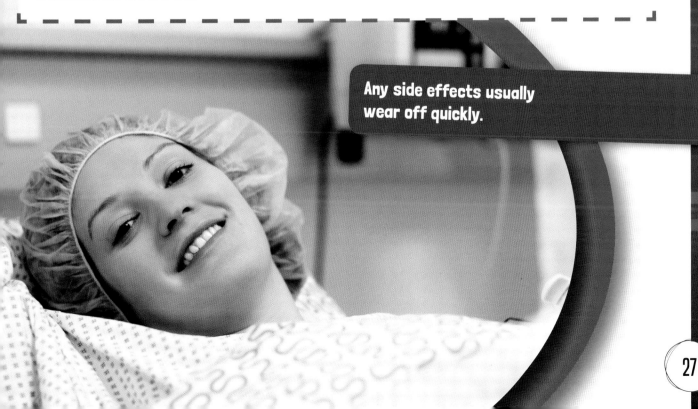

Any side effects usually wear off quickly.

ANAESTHETICS IN THE FUTURE

The world of medicine is constantly changing and **RESEARCH** is continuing into the use of anaesthetic drugs and techniques and how they work. Let's look at are some of the areas where important research is needed or is already taking place...

Scientists are looking at the ways in which anaesthetic drugs might affect the cells of patients suffering from a serious disease called cancer. They are also researching how different mixtures of anaesthetic drugs might improve survival rates for these patients.

It is known that anaesthetic drugs can affect a patient's **IMMUNE SYSTEM**. They can, for example, damage the effectiveness of the tiny hairs called cilia that are found in the respiratory system. Cilia trap and remove dust, dirt and germs in the air we breathe in. Further research in this area is needed.

RESEARCH SCIENTISTS

Research is being carried out to find out how a patient's **GENES** might affect how they react to different anaesthetic drugs. Further research is looking at the best ways to anaesthetise patients with very rare diseases.

Although anaesthetics have been used for centuries, more research is needed to find out exactly how they work and how a patient loses consciousness under a general anaesthetic. Scans that provide images of the brain are being used to show which areas of the brain are affected by anaesthetics.

Maybe you or someone in your family or class has ADHD (attention deficit hyperactivity disorder). People with ADHD are super-active and might have problems concentrating, listening and carrying out instructions. Anaesthetising children with ADHD can be difficult and more research is needed.

There are many advantages if patients can be woken up quickly after a general anaesthetic. Patients may suffer fewer side effects and take up less valuable time in the operating theatre. Research has shown that the medication commonly used to treat ADHD, Ritalin, wakes up anaesthetised rats almost immediately. Research is now being done to see if this is also the case for humans.

FASCINATING FACTS

Before anaesthetics became available, some surgeons rubbed stinging nettles onto the arms of their patients, to distract them from the pain of surgery. Others administered a hard blow to the patient's jaw, making them unconscious. Ouch!

It used to be thought that people with red hair required higher doses of anaesthetic drugs than other patients. It has now been proved that this is not true.

Injected anaesthetics are given using a hypodermic syringe – a syringe attached to a hollow needle. In 1853, French vet Charles Pravaz and Scottish doctor Alexander Wood invented the first medical hypodermic syringe. In 1956, New Zealand doctor and vet Colin Murdoch invented the first disposable plastic syringe.

The plunger is pulled back to draw the medication into the syringe and is pushed down to inject the medication through the hollow needle.

Look back to page 8. Do you remember how dwale, the primitive anaesthetic used in medieval times, contained lettuce? In the children's story, The Tale of the Flopsy Bunnies, by Beatrix Potter, the bunnies fall asleep after eating too many lettuces. The effect of eating them is described as 'soporific', which means something that makes you sleepy.

GLOSSARY

ALLERGIES unwanted reactions to substances that are harmless to most people

APPARATUS equipment or machinery needed for a particular purpose

CARBON DIOXIDE a colourless gas that is found in the atmosphere and which we breathe out when exhaling

CATARACT a medical problem in which the lens of the eye becomes misty, leading to blurred vision

CELLS the basic building blocks that make up all living things

CONSCIOUSNESS the state of being awake and aware of one's surroundings

CRIMEAN WAR a 19th century conflict (1853–1856) fought by Great Britain, France, Turkey and Sardinia against Russia

ETHER a colourless liquid that can easily be evaporated into an anaesthetic gas

GENES small parts inside cells which have information on how to make specific parts of the body, such as hair or eye colour

HEALTHCARE PROFESSIONALS doctors, nurses and other trained specialists who provide treatment for patients

HEART RATE the number of times a heart beats per minute

IMMUNE SYSTEM the organs and processes of the body that give protection against infections and toxins

INDUCED COMA a temporary coma (state of deep unconsciousness) deliberately brought on by the use of anaesthetic drugs

LATEX a rubber-like substance

LIFESTYLE the way in which a person chooses to live

MICROSCOPE a piece of scientific equipment used to look at very tiny objects by making them appear many times bigger

NITROUS OXIDE a colourless gas which, when inhaled, has an anaesthetic effect and sometimes makes the person inhaling it laugh

OBSTETRICIAN a doctor specially trained to deal with childbirth and the care of women giving birth

ORGAN a part of an organism with a specific, important function, for example the brain

OXYGEN a natural gas that most living things need in order to survive

PHARMACY a shop where medical drugs are dispensed and sold

PROTEINS organic compounds that are an essential part of all living organisms

RESEARCH investigations and experiments carried out to discover new facts

SEDATE make someone feel sleepy and relaxed by the use of anaesthetic drugs

SPINAL CORD a major part of the central nervous system that carries 'messages' to and from the brain

STERILE totally clean, free from bacteria

STIMULUS something that produces a particular reaction in the body

SURGEON a medical doctor who is qualified to carry out operations

SURGERY medical operations to repair, replace or remove damaged or diseased parts of the body

TOXIC poisonous, harmful

TRANSPLANTATION the process of taking an organ or living tissue from one person and implanting it into the body of another person

VOLATILE easily evaporated from a liquid to a gas at normal temperatures

WINDPIPE the air passage that leads from the throat to the lungs

WORLD HEALTH ORGANIZATION a group of people that look into diseases and illnesses that affect the world

INDEX